LIVING FOSSILS

# Jellyfish

Kristen Rajczak

PowerKiDS press.
New York

Published in 2015 by The Rosen Publishing Group, Inc.
29 East 21st Street, New York, NY 10010



First Edition

Editor: Sarah Machajewski
Book Design: Mickey Harmon

Photo Credits: Cover, pp. 18–19 (jellyfish) Edwin Verin/Shutterstock.com; cover (logo), pp. 1–3, 4, 8–9, 10, 12, 14, 16, 20, 22–24 (background texture) Bplanet/Shutterstock.com; cover, pp. 1–24 (border texture) Markus Gann/Shutterstock.com; p. 5 De Agostini Picture Library/De Agostini/Getty Images; pp. 6–7 Michael Nolan/Robert Harding World Imagery/Getty Images; p. 8 (moon jellies) R. Gino Santa Maria/Shutterstock.com; p. 8 (lion's mane jelly) evantravels/Shutterstock.com; p. 9 (sea nettle) chbaum/Shutterstock.com; p. 9 (purple-striped jelly) Jan Zoetekouw/Shutterstock.com; p. 11 stephan kerkhofs/Shutterstock.com; p. 13 Pavel Vakrushev/Shutterstock.com; p. 15 David Doubilet/National Geographic/Getty Images; pp. 18–19 (sea background) Jovana Milanko/Shutterstock.com; p. 19 (turtle) Ai Angel Gentel/Moment/Getty Images; p. 21 Michele Westmorland/The Image Bank/Getty Images; p. 22 Ethan Daniels/Shutterstock.com.

Library of Congress Cataloging-in-Publication Data

Rajczak, Kristen, author.
Jellyfish / Kristen Rajczak.
pages cm. — (Living fossils)
Includes index.
ISBN 978-1-4777-5827-4 (pbk.)
ISBN 978-1-4777-5829-8 (6 pack)
ISBN 978-1-4777-5832-8 (library binding)
1. Jellyfishes—Juvenile literature. 2. Living fossils—Juvenile literature. I. Title.
QL377.S4R35 2015
593.5'3—dc23

2014028311

Manufactured in the United States of America

CPSIA Compliance Information: Batch #CW15PK: For Further Information contact Rosen Publishing, New York, New York at 1-800-237-9932

# Contents

# Truly Old

In 2007, scientists found a fossil, or hardened remains, of a jellyfish that was more than 500 million years old. Up until then, scientists thought jellyfish had only been around for about 300 million years. This discovery changed everything. It showed us that jellyfish are more than two times as old as the first dinosaurs!

Unlike dinosaurs, though, jellyfish are still around. You can find them in oceans all over the world. In spite of their name, jellyfish aren't fish. They belong to the same group of sea animals as coral and sea anemones.

## FOSSIL FACTS

**Jellyfish, sea anemones, and coral are part of the animal group Cnidaria (nih-DEHR-ee-uh). The name comes from the Greek word for a stinging plant called a nettle, so it may not surprise you that all these animals can sting!**

The jellyfish that left behind these remains lived hundreds of millions of years ago.

# Oceans Worldwide

Jellyfish, or "jellies" as they're often called, have been around for hundreds of millions of years because they can survive in many kinds of water. They live in both warm and cold waters. Jellyfish are most commonly found in **shallow** water near coasts, but they can also live in very deep water. Some live in water deeper than 12,000 feet (3,658 m)!

Scientists have found about 4,000 species, or kinds, of jellyfish. They think there could be more than that. Around 200 of these species are called "true" jellyfish. They're what most people imagine when they think of jellyfish.

This jellyfish was found swimming in the icy waters near Antarctica.

## FOSSIL FACTS

Most jellyfish live in salt water, but a few live in freshwater.

# North American Jellyfish

Of the many species of jellyfish, one of the best known is the lion's mane jellyfish. It lives in the northern Atlantic and the northern Pacific Oceans. The lion's mane jellyfish is the biggest species of jellyfish in the world.

lion's mane jellyfish

moon jellies

Moon jellies are also found in the oceans around North America. They like life in calm bays and harbors. Though their name doesn't say so, sea nettles are jellyfish, too. They're found along the West Coast of the United States and Canada, along the East Coast, and in the Indian Ocean. The purple-striped jelly lives off the California coast.

sea nettle

purple-striped jelly

These are just a few examples of the thousands of jellyfish species in the world.

# The Jellyfish Body

The earliest jellies were the first animals to have **organized** body **tissues** and a **nervous system**. They were also the first animals to swim using **muscles** instead of just drifting with the ocean waves.

Jellyfish bodies are very simple. The largest part of the body is called the bell because of its shape. It's made of jellylike goo between two thin **layers** of skin. An opening in the bell is used as the jellyfish's mouth and as a way to get rid of waste. Jellyfish shoot water from their mouth to help them move through the water!

## FOSSIL FACTS

Jellyfish don't have bones, so their fossils are rare. Jellyfish fossils are actually **impressions** of their bodies, which were **preserved** in sand long ago.

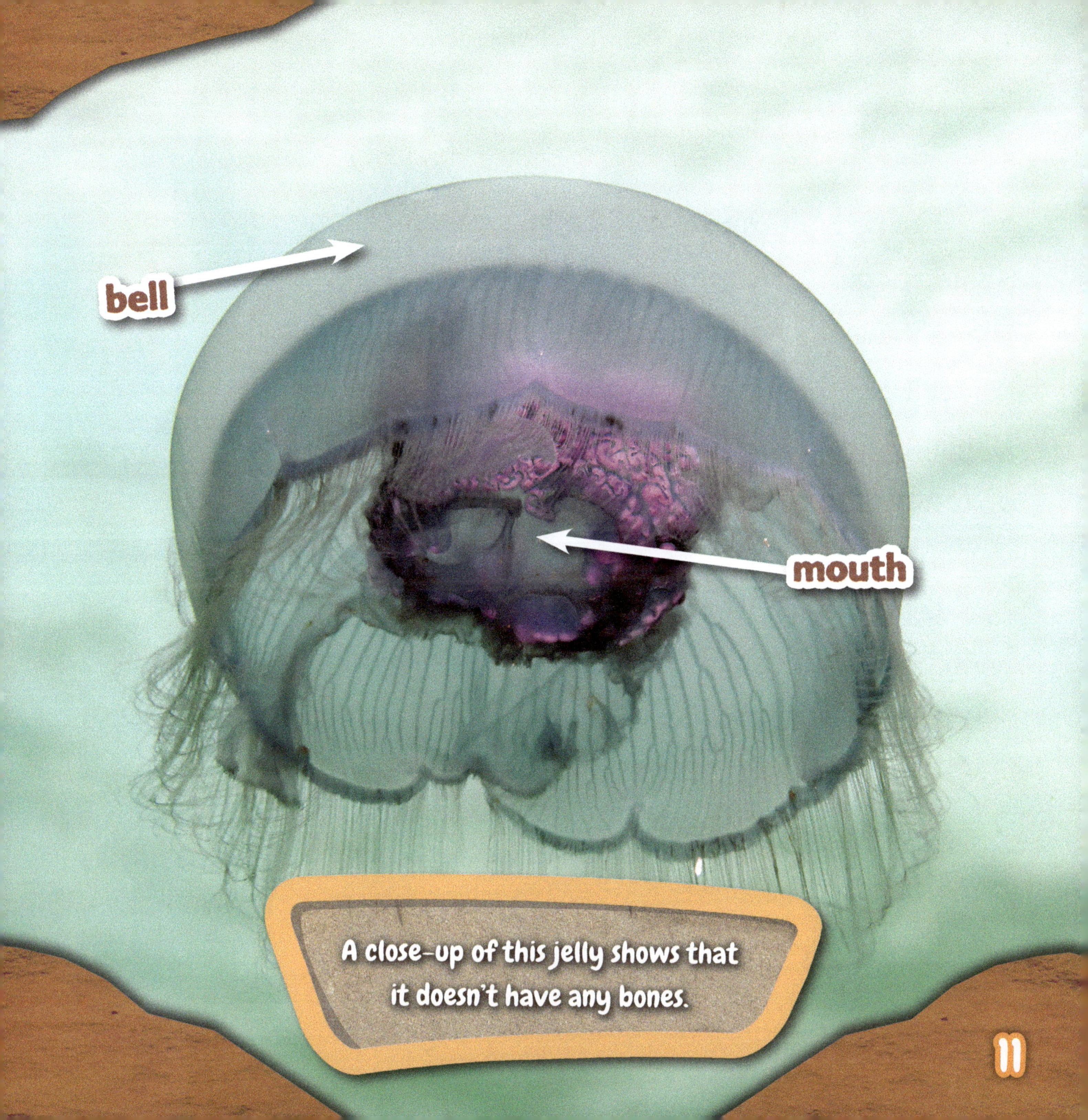


A close-up of this jelly shows that it doesn't have any bones.

# The Sting

If jellyfish are known for one thing, it's their long **tentacles**. Some species have tentacles that are 100 feet (30.5 m) long! The tentacles may look cool, but they're not safe to touch.

Jellyfish tentacles have hundreds or thousands of special stinging **cells**. Each cell contains a tiny thread that's full of **venom**. The thread leaves the cell when the tentacle touches something.

Jellyfish sting to catch food and to protect themselves from harm. Some jellyfish are more venomous than others. The box jellyfish has more than 5,000 stinging cells on its tentacles!

This Pacific sea nettle has 24 maroon tentacles. The white spirals are called oral arms.

tentacles
oral arms

# Ocean Chow

Jellyfish are carnivores, which means they eat meat. They eat tiny animals that drift in the ocean, but they also eat fish, crabs, and sometimes even larger animals. They'll eat just about anything they can catch, including other jellyfish!

A jellyfish's tentacles hang below the bell. If prey swims or floats through the tentacles, the jellyfish stings it. The stinging cells kill or **paralyze** the prey.

Once the prey is within the jellyfish's grasp, small tentacles near the mouth bring the food into its body. Jellyfish break down their food pretty quickly. It's hard to swim with a full bell!

**FOSSIL FACTS**

**Some jellyfish change colors based on what they eat! Moon jellies might look orange after they've eaten shrimp.**

This box jellyfish, also known as a sea wasp or marine stinger, uses its venomous tentacles to catch its prey.

# The Life of a Jelly

The life of a jellyfish begins with **spawning**. Female jellyfish let out eggs, and male jellyfish let out special cells. The eggs and cells join, then float in the ocean until they find something hard to stick to. There, they grow into polyps. A polyp looks like a tube with tiny tentacles at the top.

The next step could be budding, which is when a polyp makes an exact copy of itself. The polyp could also change into a jellyfish or produce a jellyfish by budding. Some polyps turn into towers of plate-like pieces. As each plate separates, it turns into a small jellyfish.

Polyps may stay in one place, budding, for many years. Adult jellyfish only live for about a year.

# The Life Cycle of a Jellyfish

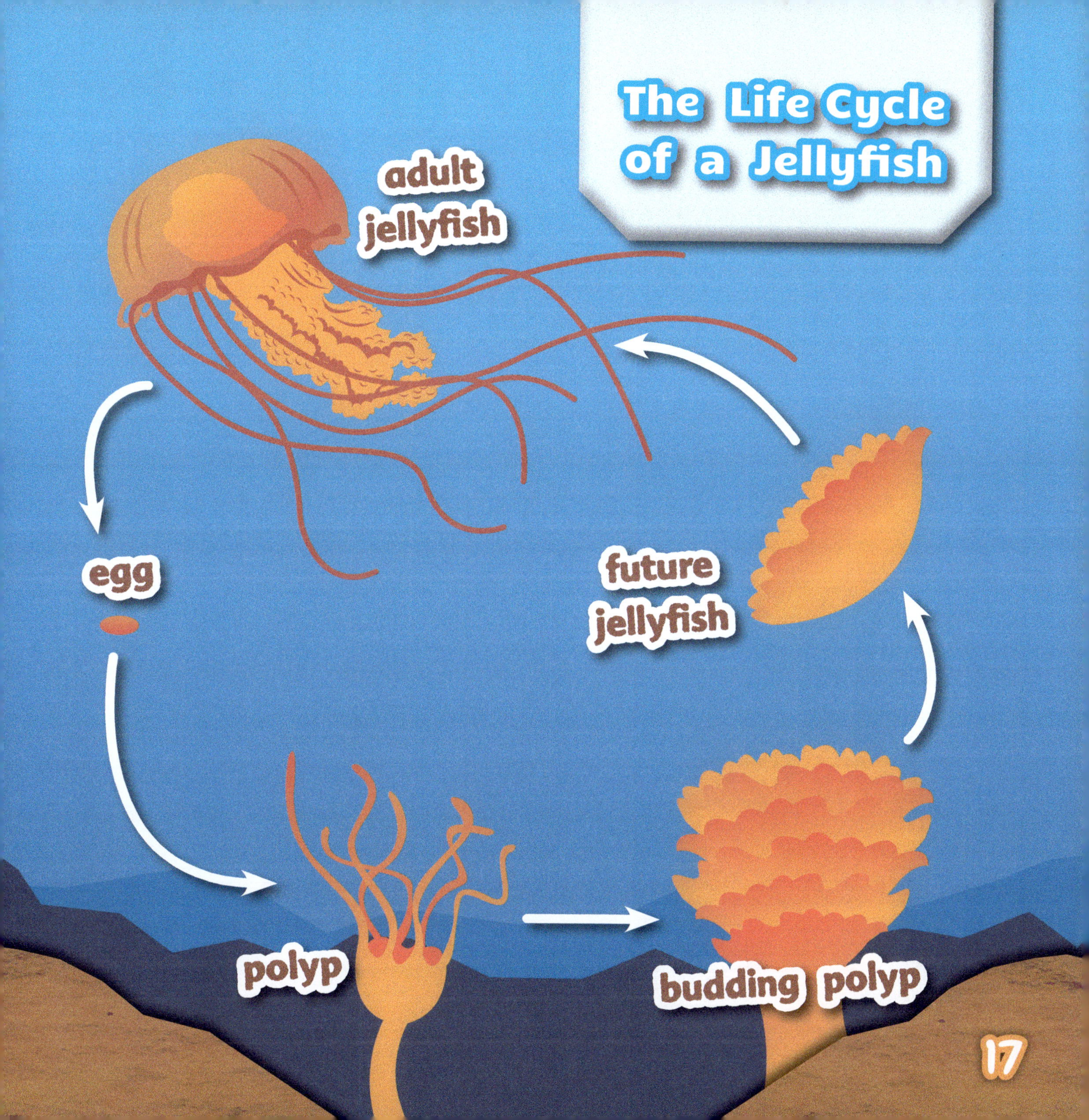

# Jellyfish Side Dish

Jellyfish may be ancient, but even the oldest animals have predators. Sea turtles like to munch on jellyfish. The leatherback sea turtle will swim for miles to find its favorite treat! Ocean sunfish are another creature that loves the taste of jellies. Baby jellyfish are so tiny that many kinds of animals end up eating them. Jellyfish have to watch out for other jellyfish, too!

Not all animals are stopped by the jellyfish's stinging tentacles!

Though jellyfish have predators, the number of jellyfish is increasing. Overfishing of some marine animals has allowed jellyfish to escape being eaten. Fewer predators means more jellyfish live—and live longer.

# Jellies and People

Jellyfish and people have shared this planet for a long time. Jellyfish have been caught off the coast of China for more than 1,700 years. Millions of pounds of jellyfish are caught each year, and eating jellyfish is becoming more common.

People are jellyfish predators, but jellies don't attack people. People who get stung by jellyfish usually swim or walk into their tentacles accidentally. How bad the sting is depends on the kind of jelly. Box jelly stings can kill people. Stings from other jellies can cause heart problems and pain for weeks. However, most jelly stings just hurt a little.

**FOSSIL FACTS**

Even the tentacles of a dead jellyfish can sting!

People can swim with jellyfish whose stings aren't powerful enough to harm them.

# Millions of Years

Large groups of jellyfish have been popping up all over the world, and their groups are getting bigger. This is partly because Earth's oceans are getting warmer. Jellies seem to grow better in warm water. People are building more hard objects in oceans, so polyps have more places to attach and grow. People are also overfishing ocean fish, and jellies are moving in to take their place.

The growth of jellyfish shows their great ability to live on a changing Earth. Jellyfish may be around for another 500 million years!

# Glossary

**cell:** The smallest basic part of a living thing.

**impression:** A mark left as a result of applying pressure on something.

**layer:** One thickness laying over or under another.

**muscle:** A collection of tissues that helps an animal or person move parts of their body.

**nervous system:** The network of cells that carries messages around the body.

**organized:** Arranged in a certain way.

**paralyze:** To make something lose the ability to move.

**preserve:** To keep something in its original state.

**shallow:** Not deep.

**spawning:** A way some marine animals reproduce in which eggs and male cells are let loose in the water.

**tentacle:** A long, thin body part that hangs from an animal's head or mouth.

**tissue:** The type of matter living things are made of.

**venom:** Something an animal makes in its body that can harm other animals.

# Index



# Websites

Due to the changing nature of Internet links, PowerKids Press has developed an online list of websites related to the subject of this book. This site is updated regularly. Please use this link to access the list: www.powerkidslinks.com/fos/jell